One Day Quilts

One Day Quilts

Beautiful Projects with NO Curved Seams

by Suzanne McNeill

Design Originals

an Imprint of Fox Chapel Publishing

www.d-originals.com

ISBN 978-1-57421-729-2

One Day Quilts (ISBN 978-1-57421-729-2, 2014) is a revised, updated, and expanded reprint of *Twist & Turn* (ISBN 978-1-57421-693-6, 2010), published by New Design Originals.

© 2010, 2014 by Suzanne McNeill and New Design Originals Corporation, www.d-originals.com, an imprint of Fox Chapel Publishing, 800-457-9112, 1970 Broad Street, East Petersburg, PA 17520.

Printed in China
First printing

One Day Quilts

Do you love the look of waves but hate the idea of sewing curves? Most quilters are just like you.

I love the flow and movement that curves add to a design, but who has time for pinning and carefully sewing curved surfaces together? Fast techniques can speed cutting and aid sewing in a jiffy.

The Twist & Turn technique makes it possible to create graceful curves by folding magic points. The last step makes the curve with easy topstitching. It's amazing and it's fun.

Don't be intimidated by designs that look complicated. Even novice quilters will enjoy success. This technique really is magical, allowing you to make curved pinwheels, interlocking tiles, hourglasses, and zig-zag designs in an endless variety of combinations.

You probably know that intricate looking patterns are receiving a lot of attention at shops, guilds, classes and shows. It seems like everybody is interested in new ways to use fabrics.

I hope you enjoy this wonderful technique with 'perfect points' and 'no curved seams'. Happy Quilting,

How to Make Perfect Points

Fold the Points
1. Fold a ¼" hem on one long side of each rectangle. Press the hem to make a finished edge.

2. Make the second fold on the diagonal. Fold one corner to the bottom center and line up the bottom edges. Press.

3. Make the third fold on the diagonal. Fold the other corner to the bottom center. Press.

4. Both folded edges should meet in the center. This will form a triangle - either large or small.

Match Triangles to Backgrounds

Match points to background blocks.
Position the long side of the triangle on the edge of the square.
Pin in place. Optional - Topstitch to baste ⅛" from the raw edge.
illustrated instructions are on pages 20-21

Secure the Edges of Each Point

5. **Option 1 - Straight Edges**
   Position and pin the triangle/s on a background square.
   Topstitch the straight edges of the triangle.

5. **Option 2 - Curved Edges**
   Position and pin the triangle/s on a background square. Gently 'roll' the edge of the triangle/s to form a curve.
   Pin in place. Topstitch the curved edges of the triangle.

Index of Quilts

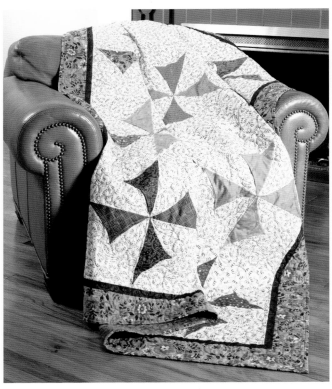

Windmills
photo pages 8-9
instructions pages 26-27

Awesome Hourglass
photo pages 10-11
instructions pages 28-29

Mother Earth
photo pages 12-13
instructions page 30-31

Cool Water
photo pages 14-15
instructions page 32-33

Fandango
photo page 16
instructions pages 34-35

Twister
photo pages 42-43
instructions page 36-37

Beauty from the Attic
photo pages 44-45
instructions page 38-39

Center Panel Quilt
photo pages 46-47
instructions pages 40-41

Windmills

pieced by Donna Perrotta
quilted by Julie Lawson

Swirling colors dance into your sewing room promising a lighthearted quilting adventure. Easy big blocks make this a great project for groups and children. The scrappy windmills give you an opportunity to hunt through your stash for those special leftover fabrics.

Your family will enjoy seeing bits of their favorite shirts or dresses spinning gracefully across this quilt. Celebrate the joy of quilting by sewing a treasure that your family will love.

instructions on pages 26 - 27

Awesome Hourglass

pieced by Lanelle Herron
quilted by Susan Corbett

Is your hourglass running on empty? Capture the sands of time and store them in a quilt that takes no time at all.

Making the Awesome Hourglass quilt is so fast, you'll have time enough to sew several! Keep this one in mind when making your holiday gift list. Your family will appreciate the energy in the design and the fashionable color palette is sure to complement any decor.

Entertain your busy quilt bee or scout troop with this quick project.

instructions on pages 28 - 29

Mother Earth

pieced by Donna Hansen
quilted by Julie Lawson

Intricate tile patterns take center stage on a quilt reminiscent of M. C. Escher drawings. Create an intriguing pattern with simple small points and give two-color quilts a fresh appeal.

instructions on pages 30 - 31

Cool Water

pieced by Kayleen Allen
quilted by Sue Needle

Soothe your soul with a comfy quilt awash in the inviting aqua shades of the ocean. You can almost smell the salty tropical breezes. Inhale deeply and let your eyes wander across the fabric surface, imagining a secluded beachfront vacation.

Just looking at this quilt will lower your blood pressure as Cool Water turns your favorite chair into a tranquil escape. Welcome home. It's time to relax.

instructions on page 32 - 33

Fandango

pieced by Donna Arends Hansen
quilted by Sue Needle

Need a baby gift this afternoon? In less time than it would take to drive
to the store and purchase a gift, you can make something really special - and
you can pick fabrics to match the baby's room!

instructions on pages 34 - 35

BASIC TIPS FOR BEGINNING QUILTERS
Rotary Cutting
Rotary Cutter: Friend or Foe

A rotary cutter is wonderful and useful. When not used correctly, the sharp blade can be a dangerous tool. Follow these safety tips:

1. Never cut toward you.
2. Use a sharp blade. Pressing harder on a dull blade can cause the blade to jump the ruler and injure your fingers.
3. Always disengage the blade before the cutter leaves your hand, even if you intend to pick it up immediately.

Rotary cutters have been caught when lifting fabric, have fallen onto the floor and have cut fingers.

Basic Sewing

You now have precisely cut strips that are exactly the correct width. You are well on your way to blocks that fit together perfectly. Accurate sewing is the next important step.

Matching Edges:

1. Carefully line up the edges of your strips. Many times, if the underside is off a little, your seam will be off by ⅛". This does not sound like much until you have 8 seams in a block, each off by ⅛". Now your finished block is a whole inch wrong!
2. Pin the pieces together to prevent them shifting.

Seam Allowance:

I cannot stress enough the importance of accurate ¼" seams. All the quilts in this book are measured for ¼" seams unless otherwise indicated.

Most sewing machine manufacturers offer a Quarter-inch foot. A Quarter-inch foot is the most worthwhile investment you can make in your quilting.

Pressing:

I want to talk about pressing even before we get to sewing because proper pressing can make the difference between a quilt that wins a ribbon at the quilt show and one that does not.

Press, do NOT iron. What does that mean? Many of us want to move the iron back and forth along the seam. This "ironing" stretches the strip out of shape and creates errors that accumulate as the quilt is constructed. Believe it or not, there is a correct way to press your seams, and here it is:

1. Do NOT use steam with your iron. If you need a little water, spritz it on.
2. Place your fabric flat on the ironing board without opening the seam. Set a hot iron on the seam and count to 3. Lift the iron and move to the next position along the seam. Repeat until the entire seam is pressed. This sets and sinks the threads into the fabric.
3. Now, carefully lift the top strip and fold it away from you so the seam is on one side. Usually the seam is pressed toward the darker fabric, but often the direction of the seam is determined by the piecing requirements.
4. Press the seam open with your fingers. Add a little water or spray starch if it wants to close again. Lift the iron and place it on the seam. Count to 3. Lift the iron again and continue until the seam is pressed. Do NOT use the tip of the iron to push the seam open. So many people do this and wonder later why their blocks are not fitting together.

5. Most critical of all: For accuracy every seam must be pressed before the next seam is sewn.

Working with 'Crosswise Grain' Strips:

Strips cut on the crosswise grain (from selvage to selvage) have problems similar to bias edges and are prone to stretching. To reduce stretching and make your quilt lay flat for quilting, keep these tips in mind.

1. Take care not to stretch the strips as you sew.
2. Adjust the sewing thread tension and the presser foot pressure if needed.
3. If you detect any puckering as you go, rip out the seam and sew it again. It is much easier to take out a seam now than to do it after the block is sewn.

Sewing Bias Edges:

Bias edges wiggle and stretch out of shape very easily. They are not recommended for beginners, but even a novice can accomplish bias edges if these techniques are employed.

1. Stabilize the bias edge with one of these methods:

a) Press with spray starch.

b) Press freezer paper or removable iron-on stabilizer to the back of the fabric.

c) Sew a double row of stay stitches along the bias edge and ⅛" from the bias edge. This is a favorite technique of garment makers.

2. Pin, pin, pin! I know many of us dislike pinning, but when working with bias edges, pinning makes the difference between intersections that match and those that do not.

Building Better Borders:

Wiggly borders make a quilt very difficult to finish. However, wiggly borders can be avoided with these techniques.

1. Cut the borders on grain. That means cutting your strips parallel to the selvage edge.
2. Accurately cut your borders to the exact measure of the quilt.
3. If your borders are piece stripped from crosswise grain fabrics, press well with spray starch and sew a double row of stay stitches along the outside edge to maintain the original shape and prevent stretching.
4. Pin the border to the quilt, taking care not to stretch the quilt top to make it fit. Pinning reduces slipping and stretching.

Basic Layering Instructions

Marking Your Quilt:

If you choose to mark your quilt for hand or machine quilting, it is much easier to do so before layering. Press your quilt before you begin. Here are some handy tips regarding marking.

1. A disappearing pen may vanish before you finish.

2. Use a white pencil on dark fabrics.

3. If using a washable Blue pen, remember that pressing may make the pen permanent.

Pieced Backings:

1. Press the backing fabric before measuring.

2. If possible cut backing fabrics on grain, parallel to the selvage edges.

3. Piece 3 parts rather than 2 whenever possible, sewing 2 side borders to the center. This reduces stress on the pieced seam.

4. Backing and batting should extend at least 2" on each side of the quilt.

Creating a Quilt Sandwich:

1. Press the backing and top to remove all wrinkles.

2. Lay the backing wrong side up on the table.

3. Position the batting over the backing and smooth out all wrinkles.

4. Center the quilt top over the batting leaving a 2" border all around.

5. Pin the layers together with 2" safety pins positioned a handwidth apart. A grapefruit spoon makes inserting the pins easier. Leaving the pins open in the container speeds up the basting on the next quilt.

Basic Quilting Instructions

Hand Quilting:

Many quilters enjoy the serenity of hand quilting. Because the quilt is handled a great deal, it is important to securely baste the sandwich together. Place the quilt in a hoop and don't forget to hide your knots.

Machine Quilting:

All the quilts in this book were machine quilted. Some were quilted on a large, free-arm quilting machine and others were quilted on a sewing machine. If you have never machine quilted before, practice on some scraps first.

Straight Line Machine Quilting Tips:

1. Pin baste the layers securely.

2. Set up your sewing machine with a size 80 quilting needle and a walking foot.

3. Experimenting with the decorative stitches on your machine adds interest to your quilt. You do not have to quilt the entire piece with the same stitch. Variety is the spice of life, so have fun trying out stitches you have never used before as well as your favorite stand-bys.

Free Motion Machine Quilting Tips:

1. Pin baste the layers securely.

2. Set up your sewing machine with a spring needle, a quilting foot, and lower the feed dogs.

Align the raw edge of the binding with the raw edge of the quilt top. Start about 8" from the corner and go along the first side with a ¼" seam.

Stop ¼" from the edge. Then stitch a slant to the corner (through both layers of binding)... lift up, then down, as you line up the edge. Fold the binding back.

Align the raw edge again. Continue stitching the next side with a ¼" seam as you sew the binding in place.

Basic Mitered Binding

A Perfect Finish:

The binding endures the most stress on a quilt and is usually the first thing to wear out. For this reason, we recommend using a double fold binding.

1. Trim the backing and batting even with the quilt edge.

2. If possible cut strips on the crosswise grain because a little bias in the binding is a Good thing. This is the only place in the quilt where bias is helpful, for it allows the binding to give as it is turned to the back and sewn in place.

3. Strips are usually cut 2½" wide, but check the instructions for your project before cutting.

4. Sew strips end to end to make a long strip sufficient to go all around the quilt plus 4"- 6".

5. With wrong sides together, fold the strip in half lengthwise. Press.

6. Stretch out your hand and place your little finger at the corner of the quilt top. Place the binding where your thumb touches the edge of the quilt. Aligning the edge of the quilt with the raw edges of the binding, pin the binding in place along the first side.

7. Leaving a 2" tail for later use, begin sewing the binding to the quilt with a ¼" seam.

For Mitered Corners:

1. Stop ¼" from the first corner. Leave the needle in the quilt and turn it 90°. Hit the reverse button on your machine and back off the quilt leaving the threads connected.

2. Fold the binding perpendicular to the side you sewed, making a 45° angle. Carefully maintaining the first fold, bring the binding back along the edge to be sewn.

3. Carefully align the edges of the binding with the quilt edge and sew as you did the first side. Repeat this process until you reach the tail left at the beginning. Fold the tail out of the way and sew until you are ¼" from the beginning stitches.

4. Remove the quilt from the machine. Fold the quilt out of the way and match the binding tails together. Carefully sew the binding tails with a ¼" seam. You can do this by hand if you prefer.

Finishing the Binding:

5. Trim the seam to reduce bulk.

6. Finish stitching the binding to the quilt across the join you just sewed.

7. Turn the binding to the back of the quilt. To reduce bulk at the corners, fold the miter in the opposite direction from which it was folded on the front.

8. Hand-sew a Blind stitch on the back of the quilt to secure the binding in place.

How to Make 'Twist & Turn' Points for 'Magic Triangles'

Cutting for Background and Points

Background Squares - cut each background block 10" x 10"
Large Points - cut each rectangle 5" x 9½"
Small Points - cut each rectangle 2¾" x 5"

How to Make Perfect Points

Fold the Points

1. Fold a ¼" hem on one long side of each rectangle. Press the hem to make a finished edge.

2. Make the second fold on the diagonal. Fold one corner to the bottom center and line up the bottom edges. Press.

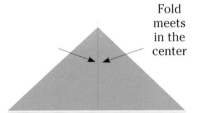

3. Fold the other corner to the bottom center. Press. Make the third fold on the diagonal.

4. Both folded edges should meet in the center. This will form a triangle - either large or small.

Match Triangles to Backgrounds

Match points to background blocks.
Position the long side of the triangle on the edge of the square.
Pin in place. Optional - Topstitch to baste ⅛" from the raw edge.

Secure the Edges of Each Point

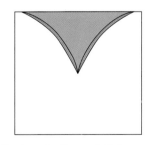

5. **Option 1 - Straight Edges**
   Position and pin the triangle/s on a background square.
   Topstitch the straight edges of the triangle.

5. **Option 2 - Curved Edges**
   Position and pin the triangle/s on a background square. Gently 'roll' the edge of the triangle/s to form a curve.
   Pin in place. Topstitch the curved edges of the triangle.

Basic Block with One Large Point

10" x 10"

Block A

Dark triangle on a light block

Block B

Light triangle on a dark block

Variations for Large Points

Basic Block with 4 Small Points

10" x 10"

Block C

Dark points on a light block

Block D

Light points on a dark block

Block E

Dark points on a light block

Block F

Light points on a dark block

Variations for Small Points

Variations for Assembly of the Large Blocks

Each Large Block will measure 19½" x 19½"

Assemble the Large Block
1. Arrange 4 squares in a large block.
2. Sew the squares together. Press.
   Each block will measure 19½" x 19½" at this point.

Blocks with Large Points

10" x 10" Blocks with One Large Point each

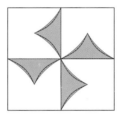

Windmills
4 of Block A
quilt on page 8-9

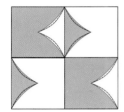

In and Out
2 each of Blocks A & B
quilt on pages 14-15

Striped Diamonds
2 each of Blocks A & B

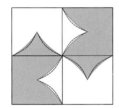

Round and Round
2 each of Blocks A & B

Design Variations for A & B

Each Large Block uses four 10" Blocks

Block G

2 Light
large points
on a dark block

Hourglass
10" Block with 2 Large Points

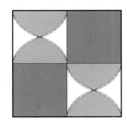

2 of Block G and
2 of an Accent Block
quilt on pages 10-11

Hourglass Variation for G

Each Large Block uses 2 of Block G and 2 Accent Blocks

Blocks with Small Points

4 of Block C

4 of Block D
quilt on pages 44-45

2 of Block E and 2 of Block F
quilt on pages 12-13

2 of Block E and 2 of an Accent Block
quilt on pages 42-43

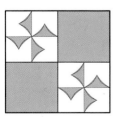

2 of small Pinwheel Block A
and 2 of an Accent Block
quilt on page 16

SIZES OF QUILTS - BASIC ASSEMBLY

Throw Quilt

SIZE: 48" x 67"

YARDAGE FOR BACKING & BATTING:
Backing   Purchase 2⅞ yards
Batting   Purchase 56" x 75"

ASSEMBLY:
   Arrange 6 large blocks on a work surface
or table.
   Sew 3 rows of 2 blocks each. Press.
   Sew the rows together. Press.

Border #1
Cut 5 strips 1½" x width of fabric.
   Cut 2 strips 1½" x 57½" for sides.
   Cut 2 strips 1½" x 40½" for top and bottom.
   Sew side borders to the quilt. Press.
   Sew top and bottom borders to the quilt. Press.

Border #2
Cut 4½" strips parallel to the selvage to
prevent piecing.
   Cut 2 strips 4½" x 59½" for sides.
   Cut 2 strips 4½" x 48½" for top and bottom.
   Sew side borders to the quilt. Press.
   Sew top and bottom borders to the quilt. Press.

Quilting
   Refer to the General Instructions and quilt
as desired.

Binding
   Cut strips 2½" wide.
   Sew strips together end to end to equal 240".

Throw Quilt Assembly Diagram

10" x 10"

Block A
Make 48

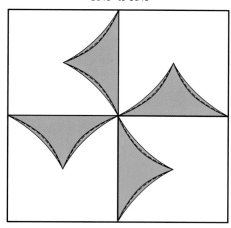

19½" x 19½"

Large Block
(sew together 4 of Block A)
Make 12

Windmills
Quilt with Large Points

photo is on pages 8 - 9

SIZE - Double Quilt
These instructions are for a Double size quilt, size 67" x 86".
   (Optional - Refer to the chart below for other sizes.)

FABRIC - We used a *Moda* "Awesome" by Sandy Gervais
   fabric collection (or use the fabric of your choice).

INSTRUCTIONS
   Refer to the chart below for yardage and cutting.
   Refer to page 20 for Blocks with Large Points.
   Block A:
    Make 48 with Large Points.
   Cut all Points from Fabric B - Medium print
   Large Blocks:
    Make 12 (each is made from 4 of Block A).
   Position the blocks to form a Pinwheel.
   Sew the blocks together in 2 rows of 2 blocks each. Press.
   Quilt Top: Sew the blocks together in 4 rows, 3 large blocks
   per row. Press.

BORDERS
   Refer to pages 22-25 for Border illustrations.
   Border #1
    Cut 7 strips 1½" x width of fabric.
     Sew together end to end. Press.
    Cut 2 strips 1½" x 76½" for sides.
    Cut 2 strips 1½" x 59½" for top and bottom.
    Sew side borders to the quilt. Press.
    Sew top and bottom borders to the quilt. Press.
   Border #2
   Cut 4½" strips parallel to the selvage to prevent piecing.
    Cut 2 strips 4½" x 78½" for sides.
    Cut 2 strips 4½" x 67½" for top and bottom.
    Sew side borders to the quilt. Press.
    Sew top and bottom borders to the quilt. Press.
   Quilting
   Refer to the Basic Instructions on pages 17-19. Quilt as desired.
   Binding
   Cut strips 2½" wide.
   Sew strips together end to end to equal 316".

Choose a Quilt Size

	Yardage		THROW SIZE	DOUBLE SIZE	KING SIZE	BABY SIZE
	Color	Location	48" x 67"	67" x 86"	113" x 113"	29" x 38½"
Fabric A	Light print	Block A Background	1¾ yards	3⅜ yards	7 yards	⅝ yard
	Or use 3 variations of Light prints, cut into 10" squares to get an assortment of Light prints for Block A					
	(⅝ yard of 3 prints - Throw Quilt, 1⅛ yard of 3 prints - Double Quilt, 2⅜ yard of 3 prints - King Quilt).					
Fabric B	Medium print	Block A Points	⅞	1¾	3⅝	⅓
	Or use one Layer Cake collection of pre-cut 10" squares to get an assortment of 24 dark prints for the points					
	(2 Layer Cakes for 48 points, 4 Layer Cakes plus 5" of border #1 for 100 points).					
Fabric C	Dark print	Border #1	¼	⅓	¾	⅙
Fabric D	Medium large print	Border #2 & Binding	1¾	2¼	3¼	⅔

	Cut Size	Location				
Block A	10" x 10"	Background	24 Light print	48 Light print	100 Light print	6 Light print
Block A	5" x 9½"	Points	24 Med. print	48 Med. print	100 Med. print	6 Med. print
		Border #1	(2) 1½" x 57½"	(2) 1½" x 76½"	(2) 2½" x 95½"	(2) 1½" x 29½"
			(2) 1½" x 40½"	(2) 1½" x 59½"	(2) 2½" x 99½"	(2) 1½" x 21½"
		Border #2	(2) 4½" x 59½"	(2) 4½" x 78½"	(2) 7½" x 99½"	(2) 4½" x 31"
			(2) 4½" x 48½"	(2) 4½" x 67½"	(2) 7½" x 113½"	(2) 4½" x 29½"

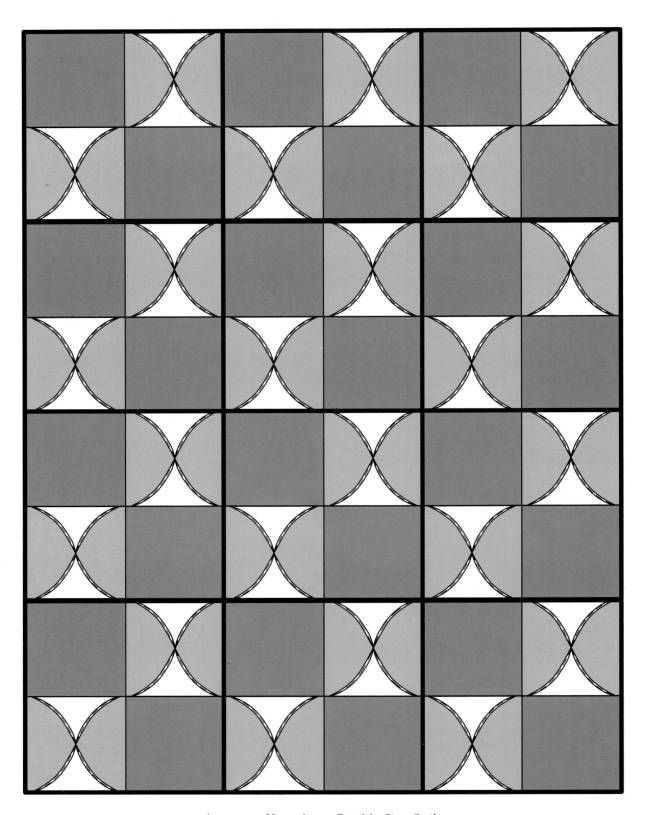

Awesome Hourglass - Double Size Quilt
see pages 22-25 for optional sizes

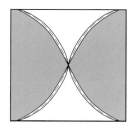

Block G
(with 2 Large Points)
Make 24

Accent Block
Cut 24

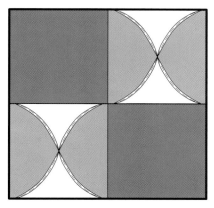

Large Block
(sew together 2 of Block G
and 2 of Accent Block)
Make 12

Awesome Hourglass
Quilt with Large Points

photo is on pages 10 - 11

SIZE - Double Quilt
These instructions are for a Double size quilt, size 67" x 86".
  (Optional - Refer to the chart below for other sizes.)

FABRIC - We used a *Moda* "Awesome" by Sandy Gervais
  fabric collection (or use the fabric of your choice).

INSTRUCTIONS
  Refer to the chart below for yardage and cutting.
  Refer to page 20 for Blocks with Large Points.
  This design uses 2 points on each background Block G.
  Block G and Accent Block:
    Make 24 of Block G with Large Points
      and 24 of the Accent Block.
  Large Blocks:
    Make 12 (each is made from 2 of Block G and
      2 of the Accent Block).
    Note the position of the blocks in each row. Press.
  Quilt Top: Sew the blocks together in 4 rows, 3 large blocks
    per row. Press.

BORDERS
  Note: The cut size of the borders listed below differ from
    pages 22-25 because this design has cornerstones.
Border #1
Cut 7 strips 1½" x width of fabric. Sew together end to end. Press.
  Cut 2 strips 1½" x 76½" for sides.
  Cut 2 strips 1½" x 59½" for top and bottom.
  Sew side borders to the quilt. Press.
  Sew top and bottom borders to the quilt. Press.
Border #2
Cut 4 Cornerstones 4½" x 4½".
Cut 4½" strips parallel to the selvage to prevent piecing.
  Cut 2 strips 4½" x 78½" for sides.
  Cut 2 strips 4½" x 59½" for top and bottom.
  Sew side borders to the quilt. Press.
  Sew a Cornerstone to each end of the top and bottom borders.
  Sew top and bottom borders to the quilt. Press.
Quilting
  Refer to the Basic Instructions on pages 17-19. Quilt as desired.
Binding
  Cut strips 2½" wide.
  Sew strips together end to end to equal 316".

Choose a Quilt Size

	Yardage					
	Color	Location	**THROW SIZE** 48" x 67"	**DOUBLE SIZE** 67" x 86"	**KING SIZE** 113" x 113"	**BABY SIZE** 29" x 38½"
Fabric A	Dark print	Accent Blocks & Cornerstones	1 yard	1⅞ yards	3⅝ yards	⅓ yard
Fabric B	Light solid	Points	⅞	1⅔	3⅝	⅓
Fabric C	Medium print	Blocks G & Border #1	1⅛	2	4¼	1
Fabric D	Medium large print	Border #2 & Binding	1¾	2¼	3¼	⅔

	Cut Size	Location				
Block A	10" x 10"	Accent Blocks	12 Dark print	24 Dark print	50 Dark print	3 Dark print
Block B	5" x 9½"	Points	24 Light Solid	48 Light Solid	100 Light Solid	6 Light Solid
Block B	10" x 10"	Background	12 Medium	24 Medium	50 Medium	3 Medium
		Cornerstones	(4) 4½" x 4½"	(4) 4½" x 4½"	(4) 7½" x 7½"	(4) 4½" x 4½"
		Border #1	(2) 1½" x 57½"	(2) 1½" x 76½"	(2) 2½" x 95½"	(2) 1½" x 29½"
			(2) 1½" x 40½"	(2) 1½" x 59½"	(2) 2½" x 99½"	(2) 1½" x 21½"
		Border #2	(2) 4½" x 59½"	(2) 4½" x 78½"	(2) 7½" x 99½"	(2) 4½" x 31"
			(2) 4½" x 40½"	(2) 4½" x 59½"	(2) 7½" x 99½"	(2) 4½" x 21½"

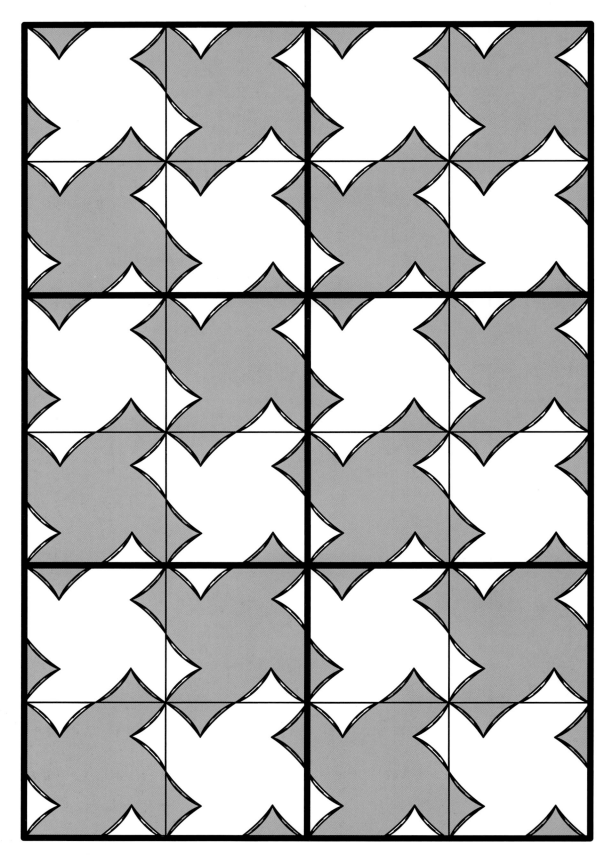

Mother Earth - Throw Size Quilt
see pages 22-25 for optional sizes

Block E
Make 12

Block F
Make 12

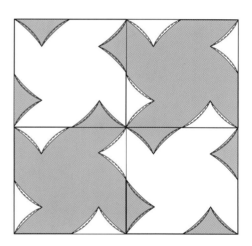

Large Block
(sew together 2 of Block E
and 2 of Block F)
Make 6

Mother Earth
Quilt with Small Points

photo is on page 10-13

SIZE - Throw Quilt

These instructions are for a Throw size quilt, size 48" x 67".
(Optional - Refer to the chart below for other sizes.)

FABRIC - We used a *Moda* "Pure" by Sweetwater
fabric collection (or use the fabric of your choice).

INSTRUCTIONS
Refer to the chart below for yardage and cutting.
Refer to page 20 for Blocks with Small Points.
This design uses 4 points on each background Block E and F.
Block E: Make 12 of Block E with 4 Small dark Points.
Block F: Make 12 of Block F with 4 Small light Points
Large Blocks:
Make 6 blocks, each using 2 of Block E and 2 of Block F.
Quilt Top: Sew the blocks together in 3 rows, 2 large blocks
per row. Press.

BORDERS
Refer to pages 22-25 for Border illustrations.
Border #1
Cut 6 strips 1½" x width of fabric. Sew together end to end. Press.
Cut 2 strips 1½" x 57½" for sides.
Cut 2 strips 1½" x 40½" for top and bottom.
Sew side borders to the quilt. Press.
Sew top and bottom borders to the quilt. Press.
Border #2
Cut 4½" strips parallel to the selvage to prevent piecing.
Cut 2 strips 4½" x 59½" for sides.
Cut 2 strips 4½" x 48½" for top and bottom.
Sew side borders to the quilt. Press.
Sew top and bottom borders to the quilt. Press.
Quilting
Refer to the Basic Instructions on pages 17-19. Quilt as desired.
Binding
Cut strips 2½" wide.
Sew strips together end to end to equal 240".

Choose a Quilt Size

	Yardage		THROW SIZE	DOUBLE SIZE	KING SIZE	BABY SIZE
	Color	Location	48" x 67"	67" x 86"	113" x 113"	29" x 38½"
Fabric A	Light print #1	Block E & Block F Points	1½ yards	2⅞ yards	5¾ yards	⅝ yard
Fabric B	Dark print #1	Block F & Block E Points	1½	2⅞	5¾	⅝
Fabric C	Dark print #2	Border #1	¼	⅓	¾	⅙
Fabric D	Light print #2	Border #2 & Binding	1¾	2¼	3¼	⅔
	Cut Size	**Location**				
Block E	10" x 10"	Background	12 Light	24 Light	50 Light	3 Light
Block E	2¾" x 5"	Points	48 Dark	96 Dark	200 Dark	12 Dark
Block F	10" x 10"	Background	12 Dark	24 Dark	50 Dark	3 Dark
Block F	2¾" x 5"	Points	48 Light	96 Light	200 Light	12 Light
		Border #1	(2) 1½" x 57½"	(2) 1½" x 76½"	(2) 2½" x 95½"	(2) 1½" x 29½"
			(2) 1½" x 40½"	(2) 1½" x 59½"	(2) 2½" x 99½"	(2) 1½" x 21½"
		Border #2	(2) 4½" x 59½"	(2) 4½" x 78½"	(2) 7½" x 99½"	(2) 4½" x 31"
			(2) 4½" x 48½"	(2) 4½" x 67½"	(2) 7½" x 113½	(2) 4½" x 29½"

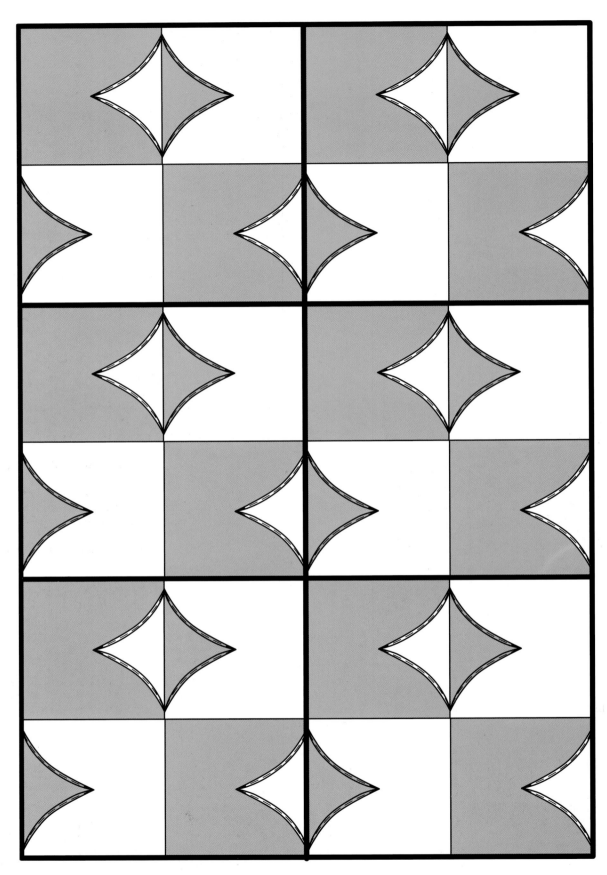

Cool Water - Throw Size Quilt
see pages 22-25 for optional sizes

Block A
Make 12

Block B
Make 12

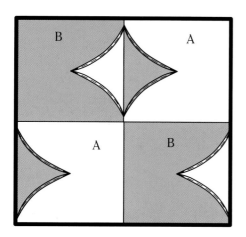

Large Block
(sew together 2 of
Block A and 2 of Block B)
Make 6

Cool Water
Quilt with Large Points
photo is on pages 14 - 15

SIZE - Throw Quilt
These instructions are for a Throw size quilt, size 48" x 67".
  (Optional - Refer to the chart below for other sizes.)

FABRIC - We used a *Moda* "Fandango" by Kate Spain
  fabric collection (or use the fabric of your choice).

INSTRUCTIONS
  Refer to the chart below for yardage and cutting.
  Refer to page 20 for Blocks with Large Points.
  Block A and Block B:
    Make 24 with Large Points.
    (12 of Block A and 12 of Block B)
  Large Blocks:
    Make 6 (each is made from 2 of Block A and 2 of Block B).
    Note the position of the blocks in each row. Press.
  Quilt Top: Sew the blocks together in 3 rows, 2 large blocks
    per row. Press.

BORDERS
  Refer to pages 22-25 for Border illustrations.

Border #1
Cut 5 strips 1½" x width of fabric.
  Cut 2 strips 1½" x 57½" for sides.
  Cut 2 strips 1½" x 40½" for top and bottom.
  Sew side borders to the quilt. Press.
  Sew top and bottom borders to the quilt. Press.

Border #2
Cut 4½" strips parallel to the selvage to prevent piecing.
  Cut 2 strips 4½" x 59½" for sides.
  Cut 2 strips 4½" x 48½" for top and bottom.
  Sew side borders to the quilt. Press.
  Sew top and bottom borders to the quilt. Press.

Quilting
  Refer to the Basic Instructions on pages 17-19. Quilt as desired.

Binding
  Cut strips 2½" wide.
  Sew strips together end to end to equal 240".

Choose a Quilt Size

	Yardage		THROW SIZE	DOUBLE SIZE	KING SIZE	BABY SIZE
	Color	Location	48" x 67"	67" x 86"	113" x 113"	29" x 38½"
Fabric A	Light print #1	Block A Background	⅞ yard	1¾ yards	3⅝ yards	⅓ yard
Fabric B	Medium print #1	Block A Points, Border #2 & Binding	1¾	2½	5⅓	1
Fabric C	Medium print #2	Block B Background	⅞	1¾	3⅝	⅓
Fabric D	Light print #2	Block B Points	½	⅞	2	⅓
Fabric E	Light small print	Border #1	¼	⅓	¾	⅙

	Cut Size	Location				
Block A	10" x 10"	Background	12 Light print #1	24 Light print #1	50 Light print #1	3 Light print #1
Block A	5" x 9½"	Points	12 Med. print #1	24 Med. print #1	50 Med. print #1	3 Med. print #1
Block B	10" x 10"	Background	12 Med. print #2	24 Med. print #2	50 Med. print #2	3 Med. print #2
Block B	5" x 9½"	Points	12 Light print #2	24 Light print #2	50 Light print #2	3 Light print #2
		Border #1	(2) 1½" x 57½"	(2) 1½" x 76½"	(2) 2½" x 95½"	(2) 1½" x 29½"
			(2) 1½" x 40½"	(2) 1½" x 59½"	(2) 2½" x 99½"	(2) 1½" x 21½"
		Border #2	(2) 4½" x 59½"	(2) 4½" x 78½"	(2) 7½" x 99½"	(2) 4½" x 31"
			(2) 4½" x 48½"	(2) 4½" x 67½"	(2) 7½" x 113½"	(2) 4½" x 29½"

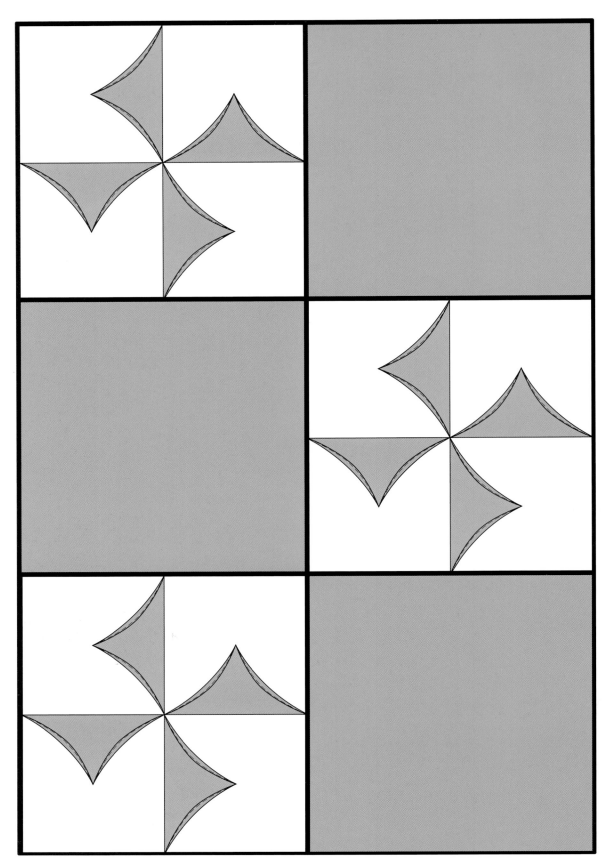

Fandango - Newborn Baby Size Quilt
see chart opposite for optional sizes

Mini Block A
Make 12

Accent Block
Cut 3
9½" x 9½"

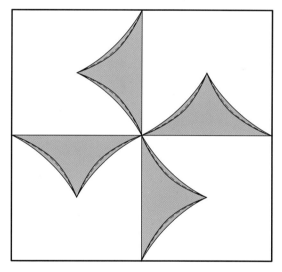

Small Pinwheel Block A
Make 3

Fandango
Quilt with Small Points

photo is on page 16

SIZE - Newborn Baby Quilt
These instructions are for a Baby size quilt, size 28" x 37".
   (Optional - Refer to the chart below for other sizes.)
FABRIC - We used a *Moda* "Fandango" by Kate Spain
   fabric collection (or use the fabric of your choice).
   Note: We used a Charm Pak of pre-cut 5" squares to get an
   assortment of 12 Medium prints for Block B.
INSTRUCTIONS
   Refer to the chart below for yardage and cutting.
   Refer to page 20 for Blocks with Small Points.
      Note: This design uses 1 Small Point on each 5" background square.
      When making the larger size quilts (throw, double, king), each
      square on the Assembly diagram represents an 18½" x 18½"
      square. Each 18½" square uses 2 Small Pinwheel blocks and
      2 Accent blocks.
   Mini Block A:
      Make 12 with Small Points on 5" background squares.
   Pinwheel Block:
      Arrange 4 of Mini Block A in a pinwheel design.
      Sew 2 rows of 2 squares each to make a 9½" x 9½" Pinwheel.
      Press. Make 3 of the Pinwheel Block.
   Accent Block: Cut 3 Accent Blocks 9½" x 9½".
   Quilt Top: Sew the blocks together in 3 rows, 2 large blocks
      per row. Press.
BORDERS
   Refer to pages 22-25 for Border illustrations.
   Note: The quilt borders will vary slightly because these blocks
      are 9½" x 9½" instead of 10" x 10".
Border #1
Cut 3 strips 1½" x width of fabric.
   Cut 2 strips 1½" x 27½" for sides.
   Cut 2 strips 1½" x 20½" for top and bottom.
   Sew side borders to quilt. Press. Sew top and bottom borders. Press.
Border #2
Cut strips 4½" x width of fabric.
   Cut 2 strips 4½" x 29½" for sides.
   Cut 2 strips 4½" x 28½" for top and bottom.
   Sew side borders to quilt. Press. Sew top and bottom borders. Press.
Quilting Refer to Basic Instructions on pages 17-19. Quilt as desired.
Binding
   Cut strips 2½" wide. Sew strips together end to end to equal 140".

Choose a Quilt Size

	Yardage		THROW SIZE	DOUBLE SIZE	KING SIZE	BABY SIZE
	Color	Location	46" x 64"	64" x 82"	108" x 108"	28" x 37"
Fabric A	Dark print	Accent Block and Points	1½ yards	2⅜ yards	5⅝ yards	⅝ yard
Fabric B	Light print	Border #1	¼	⅓	¾	⅙
Fabric C	Medium Dark print	Border #2 & Binding	1¾	2¼	3¼	⅔
Fabric D	Medium prints	Background Blocks A	⅞	1⅔	3⅝	⅓

Or use one Charm Pak collection of pre-cut 5" squares to get an assortment of medium prints for the background.
(1 Charm Pak plus 5" of border #1 for 48 squares, 3 Charm Paks for 96 squares, 5 Charm Paks for 200 squares)

	Cut Size	Location				
Block A	9½" x 9½"	Accent Blocks	12 Dark print	24 Dark print	50 Dark print	3 Dark print
Block B	2½" x 4½"	Points Block A	48 Dark print	96 Dark print	200 Dark print	12 Dark print
Block B	5" x 5"	Background Block A	48 Med. print	96 Med. print	200 Med. print	12 Med. print
		Border #1	(2) 1½" x 54½"	(2) 1½" x 72½"	(2) 2½" x 90½"	(2) 1½" x 27½"
			(2) 1½" x 38½"	(2) 1½" x 56½"	(2) 2½" x 94½"	(2) 1½" x 20½"
		Border #2	(2) 4½" x 56½"	(2) 4½" x 74½"	(2) 7½" x 94½"	(2) 4½" x 29"
			(2) 4½" x 46½"	(2) 4½" x 64½"	(2) 7½" x 108½"	(2) 4½" x 28½"

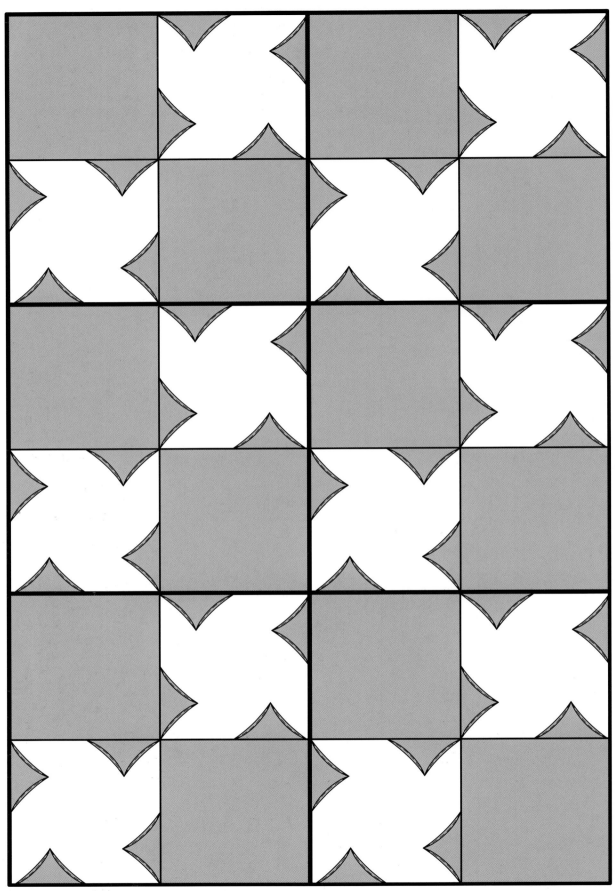

Twister - Throw Size Quilt
see pages 22-25 for optional sizes

Block E
Make 12

Accent Block
Cut 12

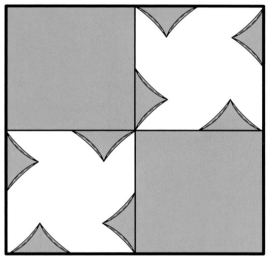

Large Block
(sew together 2 of Block E
and 2 of Accent Block)
Make 6

Twister
Quilt with Small Points

photo is on pages 42 - 43

SIZE - Throw Quilt
These instructions are for a Throw size quilt, size 48" x 67".
    (Optional - Refer to the chart below for other sizes.)
FABRIC - We used a *Moda* "Awesome" by Sandy Gervais
    fabric collection (or use the fabric of your choice).
INSTRUCTIONS
    Refer to the chart below for yardage and cutting.
    Refer to page 20 for Blocks with Small Points.
    This design uses 4 points on each background Block E.
    Block E and Accent Block:
        Make 12 of Block E with 4 Points and 12 of the Accent Block.
    Large Blocks:
        Make 6.
    Note: Each uses 2 of Block E and 2 of the Accent Block.
    Quilt Top: Sew the blocks together in 3 rows, 2 large blocks
        per row. Press.
BORDERS
    Refer to pages 22-25 for Border illustrations.
Border #1
Cut 6 strips 1½" x width of fabric. Sew together end to end. Press.
    Cut 2 strips 1½" x 57½" for sides.
    Cut 2 strips 1½" x 40½" for top and bottom.
    Sew side borders to the quilt. Press.
    Sew top and bottom borders to the quilt. Press.
Border #2
Cut 4½" strips parallel to the selvage to prevent piecing.
    Cut 2 strips 4½" x 59½" for sides.
    Cut 2 strips 4½" x 48½" for top and bottom.
    Sew side borders to the quilt. Press.
    Sew top and bottom borders to the quilt. Press.
Quilting
    Refer to the Basic Instructions on pages 17-19. Quilt as desired.
Binding
    Cut strips 2½" wide.
    Sew strips together end to end to equal 240".

Choose a Quilt Size

	Yardage		THROW SIZE	DOUBLE SIZE	KING SIZE	BABY SIZE
	Color	Location	48" x 67"	67" x 86"	113" x 113"	29" x 38½"
Fabric A	Dark print	Accent Blocks, Points & Border #1	1⅝ yards	3⅛ yards	6⅞ yards	¾ yard
Fabric B	Light print	Border #2 & Binding	1¾	2¼	3¼	⅔
Fabric C	Light print	Background Block E	⅞	1¾	3⅝	⅓

Or use 1 Layer Cake collection of pre-cut 10" squares to get an assortment of Light prints for the background Block E (1 Layer Cakes for 24 blocks - Double Quilt, 2 Layer Cakes for 50 blocks - King Quilt).

	Cut Size	Location				
Block A	10" x 10"	Accent Blocks	12 Dark print	24 Dark print	50 Dark print	3 Dark print
Block E	2¾" x 5"	Points Block E	48 Dark print	96 Dark print	200 Dark print	12 Dark print
Block E	10" x 10"	Background Block E	12 Light print	24 Light print	50 Light print	3 Light print
		Border #1	(2) 1½" x 57½"	(2) 1½" x 76½"	(2) 2½" x 95½"	(2) 1½" x 29½"
			(2) 1½" x 40½"	(2) 1½" x 59½"	(2) 2½" x 99½"	(2) 1½" x 21½"
		Border #2	(2) 4½" x 59½"	(2) 4½" x 78½"	(2) 7½" x 99½"	(2) 4½" x 31"
			(2) 4½" x 48½"	(2) 4½" x 67½"	(2) 7½" x 113½"	(2) 4½" x 29½"

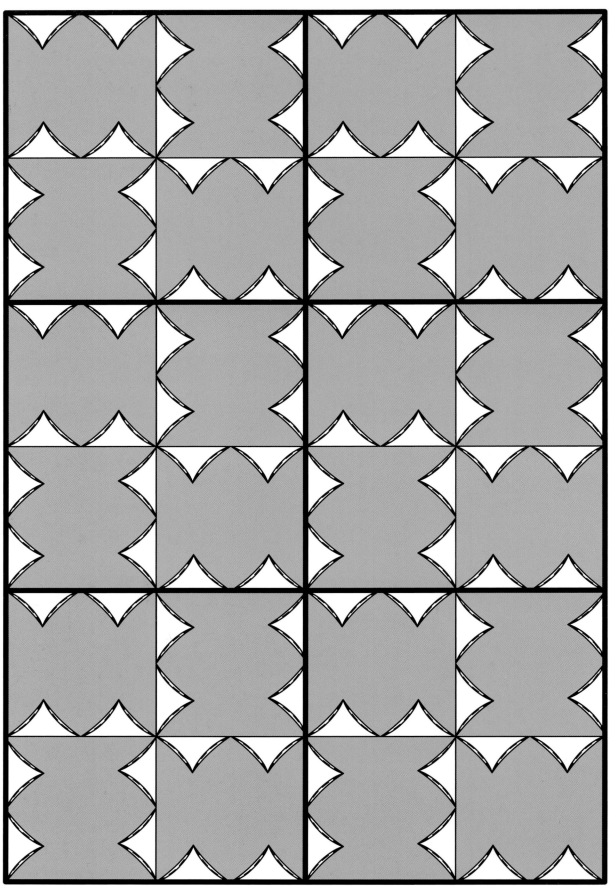

Beauty from the Attic - Throw Size Quilt
see pages 22-25 for optional sizes

Block D
Cut 24

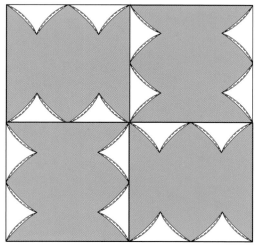

Large Block
(sew together 4 of Block D)
Make 6

Beauty from the Attic
Quilt with Small Points

photo is on pages 44 - 45

SIZE - Throw Quilt

These instructions are for a Throw size quilt, size 48" x 67".
   (Optional - Refer to the chart below for other sizes.)

FABRIC - We used a *Moda* "Arnold's Attic" by Barbara Brackman
   fabric collection (or use the fabric of your choice).

INSTRUCTIONS

   Refer to the chart below for yardage and cutting.

   Refer to page 20 for Blocks with Small Points.

   This design uses 4 points on each background Block D.

   Block D:
   Make 24 of Block D with 4 Small Points.

   Large Blocks:
   Make 6 with 4 of Block D.

   Quilt Top: Sew the blocks together in 3 rows, 2 large blocks
   per row. Press.

BORDERS

   Refer to pages 22-25 for Border illustrations.

Border #1

Cut 6 strips 1½" x width of fabric. Sew together end to end. Press.
   Cut 2 strips 1½" x 57½" for sides.
   Cut 2 strips 1½" x 40½" for top and bottom.
   Sew side borders to the quilt. Press.
   Sew top and bottom borders to the quilt. Press.

Border #2

Cut 4½" strips parallel to the selvage to prevent piecing.
   Cut 2 strips 4½" x 59½" for sides.
   Cut 2 strips 4½" x 48½" for top and bottom.
   Sew side borders to the quilt. Press.
   Sew top and bottom borders to the quilt. Press.

Quilting

   Refer to the Basic Instructions on pages 17-19. Quilt as desired.

Binding

   Cut strips 2½" wide.
   Sew strips together end to end to equal 240".

Choose a Quilt Size

	Yardage		THROW SIZE	DOUBLE SIZE	KING SIZE	BABY SIZE
	Color	Location	48" x 67"	67" x 86"	113" x 113"	29" x 38½"
Fabric A	Dark prints	Block D Background	1¾ yards	3⅜ yards	7 yards	⅝ yard
	Or use one Layer Cake collection of pre-cut 10" squares to get an assortment of Dark prints for Block D					
	(2 Layer Cakes for 48 blocks - Double Quilt, 3 Layer Cakes for 100 blocks - King Quilt)					
Fabric B	Light small print	Block D Points	1	2	4¼	⅓
Fabric C	Dark solid	Border #1	¼	⅓	¾	⅙
Fabric D	Dark print	Border #2 & Binding	1¾	2¼	3¼	⅔

	Cut Size	Location				
Block D	10" x 10"	Background	24 Dark prints	48 Dark prints	100 Dark prints	6 Dark prints
Block D	2¾" x 5"	Points	96 Light print	192 Light print	400 Light print	24 Light print
		Border #1	(2) 1½" x 57½"	(2) 1½" x 76½"	(2) 2½" x 95½"	(2) 1½" x 29½"
			(2) 1½" x 40½"	(2) 1½" x 59½"	(2) 2½" x 99½"	(2) 1½" x 21½"
		Border #2	(2) 4½" x 59½"	(2) 4½" x 78½"	(2) 7½" x 99½"	(2) 4½" x 31"
			(2) 4½" x 48½"	(2) 4½" x 67½"	(2) 7½" x 113½"	(2) 4½" x 29½"

Center Panel Print
Cut 23½" x 41½"

Border #1

Border #2

Border #3

Center Panel Quilt
Saltbox Harvest

Block H
2 Small Points
on a 4" x 9½" background piece
Make 16

Center Panel Quilt
Saltbox Harvest
Quilt with Small Points

photo is on pages 46 - 47

SIZE - Throw Quilt

These instructions are for a Throw size quilt, size 42" x 60".

FABRIC - We used a *Moda* "Saltbox Harvest" by Deb Strain
fabric collection (or use the fabric of your choice).

YARDAGE AND CUTTING:

Color	Yardage	Location
Printed Panel	23½" x 41½"	Quilt Center
Black solid	½ yard	Border #1 & Cornerstones
Ivory print	½	Border Block H
Dark Red print for Points	½	Block H Points
Black print	1½	Border #3 & Binding
Fabric for Backing	2⅓	
Batting	50" x 68"	

ASSEMBLY

Center Panel

Cut the panel 23½" x 41½".

BORDERS

Black Border #1

Cut 2 strips 2½" x 41½" for sides.

Cut 2 strips 2½" x 27½" for top and bottom.

Sew side borders to the quilt. Press.

Sew top and bottom borders to the quilt. Press.

BORDER WITH POINTS

Points Border #2

Cut 16 Ivory print 4" x 9½" rectangle border blocks H.

Cut 32 Dark Red points 2¾" x 5".

Cut 4 Black cornerstones 4" x 4".

This design uses 2 points side by side on each background block H.

Refer to page 20 for construction of Rectangles with Mini Points.

Assemble the Border

Sew 5 blocks together to make each side border 4" x 45½". Make 2. Press.

Sew 3 blocks to make the top/bottom borders 4" x 27½". Make 2. Press.

Sew a cornerstone to each end of the top and bottom borders. Press.

Sew side borders to the quilt. Press.

Sew top and bottom borders to the quilt. Press.

OUTSIDE BORDER

Black Print Border #3

Cut 4½" strips parallel to the selvage to prevent piecing.

Cut 2 strips 4½" x 52½" for sides.

Cut 2 strips 4½" x 42½" for top and bottom.

Sew side borders to the quilt. Press.

Sew top and bottom borders to the quilt. Press.

Quilting

Refer to the Basic Instructions on pages 17-19. Quilt as desired.

Binding

Cut strips 2½" wide.

Sew strips together end to end to equal 214".

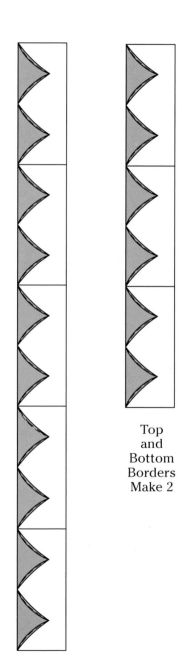

Top
and
Bottom
Borders
Make 2

Side
Borders
Make 2

Twister

pieced by Rose Ann Pegram
quilted by Susan Corbett

Round and round we go! If you enjoy creating designs with a lot of movement, Twister is destined to become a favorite.

Mixing floral patterns with a variety of prints enlivens this sassy design with modern day appeal. Small triangles create the shape and speedy construction makes this a quick and fun project.

instructions on pages 36 - 37

Beauty from the Attic

pieced by Lanelle Herron
quilted by Sue Needle

*Remember how much fun it was to rummage through Grandma's attic...
the excitement of lifting that dusty trunk lid...the rapture of discovering a
collection of her hand-made quilts!*

*Relive the adventure with fabrics reminiscent of times long past and
create a keepsake for future generations to cherish. You'll enjoy updating
Grandma's techniques with our speedy tips. Make this quilt in an afternoon.*

instructions on page 38 - 39

Center Panel Quilt

pieced by Rose Ann Pegram
quilted by Sue Needle

    Purchasing a printed panel is a lot like buying a painting. It comes with attractive images and pretty colors - all ready to frame. Too often, we never quite get around to the framing.

    One of the most popular quilt classes now being offered deals with creatively using panels - probably because quilters love them, buy them, and then stash them. We intended to turn them into something when we bought them...didn't we?

    It's time to get your favorite panels out of the stash and into a finished quilt. Our triangle technique adds a fast and fabulous border. Need it bigger? Keep adding borders.

instructions on pages 40 - 41

Suzanne McNeill

SUPPLIERS
Most quilt and fabric stores carry an excellent assortment of supplies. If you need something special, ask your local store.

COTTON FABRICS,
JELLY ROLLS,
LAYER CAKES
Moda Fabrics, United Notions
www.unitednotions.com

QUILTING BY
Julie Lawson, 817-428-5929
Sue Needle, 817-589-1168

MANY THANKS to my staff for their cheerful help and wonderful ideas!

Kathy Mason • Patty Williams
Donna Kinsey • Kristy Krouse
David & Donna Thomason

"I love designing ... painting, crafting and working with my hands. The colors, feel and textures of fabrics and textiles are exciting. Quilts are my favorite! Opening my mind to all the beautiful things in life inspires my creativity," shares Suzanne with infectious enthusiasm.

"The opportunity to visit another culture in a different time and place is always inspiring. Designs are inspired not from recording what I experience but by interpreting everything around me."

Suzanne shares her creativity in books by Design Originals.

Popular best-selling books are known for simple construction and colorful designs. Her mission is to publish books that help others learn about the newest techniques, best projects and most popular products.

Check It Out!

On the following pages you will find alternative color schemes for the quilts in this book that will show you the diverse ways your quilt could come together. Try exploring the racks of fabrics at your local store and envisioning different patterns and textures in your chosen color palette. The possibilities are practically endless.

Windmills

Color photo on pages 8 - 9
Instructions on pages 26 - 27

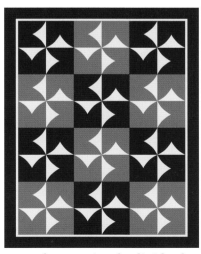

For these 3 quilts (bottom row), if you want to achieve a checkerboard pattern shown, simply divide the yardage given for fabrics A and B in half, and create 6 large blocks with half of your fabric and 6 large blocks with the other half.

Awesome Hourglass

Color photo on pages 10 - 11
Instructions on pages 28 - 29

Mother Earth

Color photo on pages 12 - 13
Instructions on pages 30 - 31

Cool Water

Color photo on pages 14 - 15
Instructions on pages 32 - 33

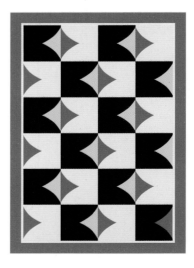

Check out the Moda fabrics used in this quilt at
www.unitednotions.com.

Fandango

Color photo on pages 16
Instructions on pages 34 - 35

Twister

Color photo on pages 42 - 43
Instructions on pages 36 - 37

Beauty from the Attic

Color photo on pages 44 - 45
Instructions on pages 38 - 39

Center Panel Quilt

Color photo on pages 46 - 47
Instructions on pages 40 - 41